THE AMAZING WORLD OF GUMBALL TRIVIA BOOK

A SPECIAL TRIVIA QUIZZES COLLECTION AND FUN FACTS FOR THE AMAZING WORLD OF GUMBALL FANS

To the people who are having this book,

We would like to thank you for choosing our product and hope you have a great time with this activity book. Therefore, if you think this book is interesting and you love it, could you please give a minute to share your thinking on Amazon. That would be so grateful to us and we appreciate your support a lot.

Thanks so much and wish you all the best.

TABLE OF CONTENT

This Brilliant Trivia Book belongs to

....

CHAPTER 1

WELCOME

LET'S QUIZZ!

1. The Amazing World of Gumball is a British-American animated sitcom.
    A. True
    B. False

2. Who is the creator of The Amazing World of Gumball?
    A. Teresa Gallagher
    B. Logan Grove
    C. Ben Bocquelet
    D. Mic Graves

3. How many seasons does The Amazing World of Gumball have?

    A. 2

    B. 4

    C. 6

    D. 8

4. How many episodes does The Amazing World of Gumball have?

    A. 210

    B. 220

    C. 230

    D. 240

5. Who is the director of The Amazing World of Gumball in season 1-4?

    A. Teresa Gallagher

    B. Antoine Perez

    C. Ben Bocquelet

    D. Mic Graves

6. Who is the director of The Amazing World of Gumball in season 5-6?

    A. Teresa Gallagher

    B. Antoine Perez

    C. Ben Bocquelet

    D. Mic Graves

7. How many episodes in season 1?

    A. 36

    B. 38

    C. 40

    D. 42

8. How many episodes in season 2?

    A. 36

    B. 38

    C. 40

    D. 42

9. How many episodes in season 3?

    A. 36

    B. 38

    C. 40

    D. 42

10. How many episodes in season 4?

    A. 36

    B. 38

    C. 40

    D. 42

11. How many episodes in season 5?

   A. 36

   B. 38

   C. 40

   D. 42

12. How many episodes in season 6?

   A. 40

   B. 42

   C. 44

   D. 46

13. When was the first aired of season 1?

   A. January 3rd, 2011

   B. March 3rd, 2011

   C. May 3rd, 2011

   D. July 3rd, 2011

14. When was the last aired of season 1?

   A. January 13th, 2012

   B. March 13th, 2012

   C. May 13th, 2012

   D. July 13th, 2012

15. When was the first aired of season 2?

    A. June 7th, 2012

    B. August 7th, 2012

    C. October 7th, 2012

    D. December 7th, 2012

16. When was the last aired of season 2?

    A. June 3rd, 2013

    B. August 3rd, 2013

    C. October 3rd, 2013

    D. December 3rd, 2013

17. When was the first aired of season 3?

    A. June 5th, 2014

    B. August 5th, 2014

    C. October 5th, 2014

    D. December 5th, 2014

18. When was the last aired of season 3?

    A. June 6th, 2015

    B. August 6th, 2015

    C. October 6th, 2015

    D. December 6th, 2015

19. When was the first aired of season 4?

   A. July 7th, 2015

   B. August 7th, 2015

   C. September 7th, 2015

   D. October 7th, 2015

20. When was the last aired of season 4?

   A. July 27th, 2016

   B. August 27th, 2016

   C. September 27th, 2016

   D. October 27th, 2016

21. When was the first aired of season 5?

   A. July 1st, 2016

   B. August 1st, 2016

   C. September 1st, 2016

   D. October 1st, 2016

22. When was the last aired of season 5?

   A. September 10th, 2017

   B. October 10th, 2017

   C. November 10th, 2017

   D. December 10th, 2017

23. When was the first aired of season 6?

    A. January 5th, 2018

    B. February 5th, 2018

    C. March 5th, 2018

    D. April 5th, 2018

24. When was the last aired of season 6?

    A. May 24th, 2019

    B. June 24th, 2019

    C. July 24th, 2019

    D. August 24th, 2019

25. The DVD is the first episode in season 1.

    A. True

    B. False

CHAPTER 1

WELCOME

ANSWERS ARE COMING!!

1. A.True

2. C.Ben Bocquelet

3. C.6

4. D.240

5. D.Mic Graves

6. B.Antoine Perez

7. A.36

8. C.40

9. C.40

10. C.40

11. C.40

12. C.44

13. C.May 3rd, 2011

14. B.March 13th, 2012

15. B.August 7th, 2012

16. D.December 3rd, 2013

17. A.June 5th, 2014

18. B.August 6th, 2015

19. A.July 7th, 2015

20. D.October 27th, 2016

21. C.September 1st, 2016

22. C.November 10th, 2017

23. A.January 5th, 2018

24. B.June 24th, 2019

25. A.True

DID YOU KNOW?

➤ According to show creator Ben Bocquelet, the name Gumball was given before the character was created because it represented the childlike nature of the show.

➤ The backgrounds of Elmore are actually photos taken of San Francisco and Vallejo, California, as well as some places in London.

CHAPTER 2

FALL IN LOVE
LET'S QUIZZ!

1. Who is Gumball in love with?

   A. Penny and himself

   B. Rio and Bob

   C. Sarah

   D. Keane

2. What happens when Anais rubs her socks together?

   A. They get dirty

   B. She transforms into someone else

   C. They generate electricity

   D. Absolutely nothing

3. What is Penny allergic to?

   A. People

   B. Water

   C. Peppers

   D. Peanuts

4. What is Gumball's real name?

   A. Richard Jr

   B. Patrick

   C. Zach

   D. Johny Bravo

5. Who does Darwin accidentally kiss in the treehouse?

   A. Penny

   B. Gumball

   C. Jackie

   D. A mirror

6. What is Gumball's biggest fear?

   A. Snakes

   B. Spiders

   C. Butterflies

   D. His mum

7. Who is Principal Brown's girlfriend?

   A. Miss Simian

   B. Yuki

   C. Mrs Robinson

   D. None of the above

8. How old is Anais Watterson?

   A. 1

   B. 2

   C. 3

   D. 4

9. What is Darwin Watterson's full name?

   A. Darwin Nicodemius Watterson III
Darwin Raglan Caspian Watterson III

   B. Darwin Raglan Caspian Nicodemius Watterson III

   C. Darwin Raglan Caspian Ahab Poseidon
Nicodemius Watterson III

10. What type of animal is Darwin?

   A. Cat

   B. horse

   C. Dog

   D. Goldfish

11. In which episode was Gumball given the nickname, GumballOopsEggWobbleUnderpants?

    A. The coat

    B. The skirt

    C. The dress

    D. Th hat

12. What job does Nicole Watterson do?

    A. Salesperson

    B. Doctor

    C. Teacher

    D. Singer

13. Which other language can Richard Watterson speak fluently?

    A. Japanese

    B. Chinese

    C. Spanish

    D. Russian

14. Who is called Clever Girl by Gumball and Richard?

    A. Miss Simian

    B. Anais

    C. Penny

    D. Nicole

15. What is Gumball's middle name?

    A. Smith

    B. Tristopher

    C. Ukulele

    D. Piano

16. What is Lucy Simian's profession?

    A. Salesperson

    B. Doctor

    C. Teacher

    D. Singer

17. Penny Fitzgerald is a shape-shifting fairy. But what was she originally?

    A. A pool float

    B. An antlered peanut

    C. A beanbag

    D. A tin

18. Who is the youngest and cleverest member of the Watterson family?

    A. Denise

    B. Clarice

    C. Anais

    D. Keith Jampot

19. Which animal is Miss Simian based on?

    A. Horse

    B. Sheep

    C. Snake

    D. Monkey

20. What is Richard Buckley Watterson's favourite food?

    A. Candy

    B. Bread

    C. Sausage

    D. Sandwich

21. Where does Nicole work?

    A. Rainbow Factory

    B. Sunny Factory

    C. Cloudy Factory

    D. Clock Wall Factory

22. What is the name of the Principal?

    A. Nigel Brown

    B. Nigel Black

    C. Nigel Red

    D. Nigel Yellow

23. What is Hot Dog Guy's hair made from?

  A. Egg

  B. Mustard

  C. Fish

  D. Banana

24. Gumball and Darwin are the only characters to appear in every single episode.

  A. True

  B. False

25. The man who created the show, Ben Bocquelet, is allergic to cats!

  A. True

  B. False

CHAPTER 2

FALL IN LOVE

ANSWERS ARE COMING!!

1. A. Penny and himself

2. C.They generate electricity

3. D.Peanuts

4. C.Zach

5. B.Gumball

6. B.Spiders

7. A.Miss Simian

8. D.4

9. C.Darwin Raglan Caspian Ahab PoseidonNicodemius Watterson III

10. D.Goldfish

11. C.The dress

12. A.Salesperson

13. C.Spanish

14. B.Anais

15. B.Tristopher

16. C.Teacher

17. B.An antlered peanut

18. C.Anais

19. D.Monkey

20. C.Sausage

21. A.Rainbow Factory

22. A. Nigel Brown

23. B.Mustard

24. A.True

25. A.True

DID YOU KNOW?

➢ The characters Anais, Richard, and Nicole Watterson are named and based on Ben Bocquelet's own family members.

➢ The van where Richard bought the Evil Turtle is also where he bought Darwin, as seen in season four, episode nineteen, "The Origins".

➢ Gumball increases in intelligence during the series.

CHAPTER 3

MY DREAM
LET'S QUIZZ!

1. Where do the Wattersons live?

    A. Elmore

    B. Somore

    C. Anymore

    D. More

2. Who's the smartest in the family?

    A. Gumball

    B. Darwin

    C. Anais

    D. Nicole

3. Which one is a robot?

   A. Bobert

   B. Louis

   C. Kary

   D. Ken

4. How old is Gumball?

   A. 10

   B. 11

   C. 12

   D. 13

5. Who was the main character in "The Boombox"?

   A. Gumball

   B. Anais

   C. Juke

   D. Darwin

6. Which episode did Gumball accidentally kiss Darwin?

   A. The Cat

   B. The Kiss

   C. The Stress

   D. The Pressure

7. What episode Richard shrink Gumballs clothes?

  A. The Procrastinators

  B. The Dress

  C. The Slide

  D. The Awkwardness

8. Which episode does TaWoG make a Tinder reference?

  A. The Crew

  B. The Dress

  C. The Slide

  D. The Awkwardness

9. Which episode does Gumball and Darwin make themselves look old?

  A. The Crew

  B. The Dress

  C. The Slide

  D. The Awkwardness

10. How old is Anais in 1st episode?

  A. 1

  B. 2

  C. 3

  D. 4

11. What will corrupt Anais' mind, according to Gumball?

   A. TV commercials

   B. Candy

   C. Drink

   D. Gumball

12. Where did Richard find the babysitter?

   A. On the magazine

   B. On the newspaper

   C. On the internet

   D. On the street

13. What does Richard set fire to?

   A. The house

   B. The school

   C. A swimming pool

   D. A library

14. What does Gumball serve for dessert in 1st episode?

   A. A dress

   B. A shoe

   C. A coat

   D. A tie

15. Which of these house object gets smashed by Gumball and Darwin?

    A. The TV

    B. The cough

    C. The cup

    D. The box

16. Where does Gumball and Darwin forbid Anais to go?

    A. Kitchen

    B. Living room

    C. Bathroom

    D. Upstairs

17. Who's Larry?

    A. A student

    B. A cardboard man

    C. A robber

    D. A brick that gets thrown in a random episode

18. Steve small a teacher.

    A. True

    B. False

19. Steve is also an artist.

   A. True

   B. False

20. What's Ocho's uncle name

   A. Ralph

   B. Ochomito

   C. Mario

   D. Max sam in

21. What did Moonchild corneille do when Joao was training to fight him?

   A. Train harder IN

   B. Relax

   C. Sing

   D. Dance

22. What animal is Gumball?

   A. Dog

   B. Fish

   C. Frog

   D. Cat

23. When Moonchild corneille was fighting Joao, who won?

   A. Moonchild

   B. Joao

24. Which one of these characters is really stupid in the Watterson family?

   A. Gumball

   B. Richard

   C. Darwin

   D. Anais

25. Who is the teacher who taught in the Stone Age?

   A. Principal Brown

   B. Rocky

   C. Miss Simian

   D. Mr. Small

CHAPTER 3

MY DREAM

ANSWERS ARE COMING!!

1. A.Elmore
2. C.Anais
3. A.Bobert
4. C.12
5. C.Juke
6. D.The Pressure
7. B.The Dress
8. C.The Slide
9. A.The Crew
10. D.4
11. A.TV commercials
12. C.On the internet
13. C.A swimming pool
14. B.A shoe
15. A.The TV
16. D.Upstairs
17. B.A cardboard man
18. A.True
19. A.True
20. C.Mario
21. B.Relax
22. D.Cat
23. B.Joao
24. A.Gumball
25. A. Principal Brown

DID YOU KNOW?

➤ Gumball has been to the hospital more than anyone else in the show.

➤ Every character in the series is hurt at least one time.

➤ The only episodes not to have the word "The" in their titles are "Halloween" and "Christmas".

➤ Darwin is not the original Watterson pet. Richard bought a total of nine fish, all of whom Gumball accidentally killed, before he bought the Darwin we all know and love.

CHAPTER 4

HOW ARE YOU?
LET'S QUIZZ!

1. What is Anais's favorite animal?

   A. Daisy

   B. Rose

   C. Tulip

   D. Cherry

2. What animal is Anais?

   A. Cat

   B. Spider

   C. Rabbit

   D. Dolphin

3. Darwin sleeps in a fish bowl

    A. True

    B. False

4. Who is the adult woman that extremely strong when she is angry?

    A. Miss Simian

    B. Nicole Watterson

    C. Mrs. Robinson

    D. Penny

5. What is Nicole's characteristic?

    A. Strong

    B. Athletic

    C. Brave

    D. All of the above

6. Who is Gumball's mom?

    A. Nicole

    B. Mairia

    C. Stella

    D. Anna

7. Gumball and Darwin are brothers and best friends but they are a bit stupid.

    A. True

    B. False

8. How old is Penny?

    A. 11

    B. 12

    C. 13

    D. 14

9. Who is the boy who has a crush on Penny?

    A. Gumball

    B. Leslie

    C. Alan

    D. Tobias

10. Which person is the laziest person in Elmore?

    A. Richard

    B. Darwin

    C. Nicole

    D. Gumball

11. Nicole will scream at you if you do anything wrong.

    A. True

    B. False

12. What color is Banana Joe?

    A. Red

    B. Blue

    C. Yellow

    D. Orange

13. What color is Anais?

    A. Black

    B. Pink

    C. Brown

    D. Yellow

14. What color is Anais's tail?

    A. White

    B. Black

    C. Brown

    D. Red

15. Tobias is a rich person.

   A. True

   B. False

16. What color is Anais's nose?

   A. White

   B. Black

   C. Brown

   D. Red

17. What color is Anais's dress that she often wears?

   A. Red

   B. Blue

   C. Yellow

   D. Orange

18. What color is Gumball?

   A. Red

   B. Blue

   C. Yellow

   D. Orange

19. Banana Joe has googly eyes.

    A. True

    B. False

20. How many whiskers does Gumball have?

    A. 2

    B. 4

    C. 6

    D. 8

21. How many Gumball's whiskers can you see?

    A. 1

    B. 3

    C. 5

    D. 7

22. What color is Gumball's trousers?

    A. Red

    B. Gray

    C. Tan

    D. Orange

23. Alongside Darwin and Granny Jojo, Anais has footwear unlike the rest of her family.

   A. True

   B. False

24. What color is Gumball's sweater?

   A. Red

   B. Gray

   C. Tan

   D. Orange

25. Gumball is a very imaginative person.

   A. True

   B. False

CHAPTER 4

HOW ARE YOU?

ANSWERS ARE COMING!!

1. A.Daisy
2. C.Rabbit
3. A.True
4. B. Nicole Watterson
5. D.All of the above
6. A.Nicole
7. A.True
8. B.12
9. D. Tobias
10. A.Richard
11. A.True
12. C.Yellow
13. B.Pink
14. A.White
15. A.True
16. D.Red
17. D.Orange
18. B.Blue
19. A.True
20. C.6
21. C.5
22. B.Gray
23. A.True
24. C.Tan
25. A.True

DID YOU KNOW?

➢ Gumball and Darwin have had four voice actors throughout the series. Anais has only had one.

➢ All of the episodes in all the series start with the word "the" for example "the name" "the guy" and "the castle"

➢ Even though Gumball is a kid's show, there are many adult jokes hidden throughout the series.

CHAPTER 5

LONG TIME NO SEE!
LET'S QUIZZ!

1. Who is Gumball's adoptive brother?

    A. Darwin

    B. Richard

    C. Louie

    D. Daniel

2. Who is Gumball's father?

    A. Darwin

    B. Richard

    C. Louie

    D. Daniel

3. What color is Darwin's pants?

   A. Pink

   B. Blue

   C. Orange

   D. He doesn't wear pants

4. Darwin can breathe in both water and air.

   A. True

   B. False

5. What kind of food does Darwin like in "The Countdown" episode?

   A. Russian food

   B. American food

   C. English food

   D. Mexican food

6. In "The Matchmaker", who is the person that Darwin has a crush on?

   A. Bee

   B. Purple

   C. Carrie

   D. Galiile

7. Darwin has a habit of standing in his seat as opposed to sitting down.

    A. True

    B. False

8. In " The Internet", what instrument is Darwin good at?

    A. Saxophone

    B. Guitar

    C. Piano

    D. Ukulele

9. What is Darwin allergic to?

    A. Beans

    B. Peanuts

    C. Feathers

    D. Potatoes

10. What animal is Nicole?

    A. Cat

    B. Dog

    C. Penguin

    D. Fish

11. What color is Nicole's fur?

    A. Brown

    B. Purple

    C. Blue

    D. Yellow

12. What color is Nicole's nose?

    A. Brown

    B. Purple

    C. Blue

    D. Pink

13. Nicole is usually barefoot.

    A. True

    B. False

14. How old is Nicole?

    A. 32

    B. 36

    C. 38

    D. 40

15. Nicole is well-known for her short temper.

    A. True

    B. False

16. Nicole and Richard's wedding anniversary is on ____

    A. September 1st

    B. October 1st

    C. November 1st

    D. December 1st

17. What type of blood is Nicole?

    A. A

    B. B

    C. AB

    D. 0

18. When is Nicole's birthday?

    A. September 12th

    B. October 12th

    C. November 12th

    D. December 12th

19. Richard is pink color.

    A. True

    B. False

20. What animal is Richard?

    A. Giraffe

    B. Dog

    C. Cat

    D. Rabbit

21. How many whiskers does Richard have?

    A. 2

    B. 4

    C. 6

    D. 8

22. What is Richard's characteristic?

    A. Childish

    B. Lazy

    C. Good intentions

    D. All of the above

23. Even though he is unemployed, Richard is almost always seen wearing a work uniform.

    A. True

    B. False

24. What is Richard's favorite food?

    A. Hotdog

    B. Sausage

    C. Pizza

    D. Sandwich

25. Richard is shown enjoying dressing like a woman in "The Finale" and "The Safety."

    A. True

    B. False

CHAPTER 5

LONG TIME NO SEE!

ANSWERS ARE COMING!!

1. A.Darwin

2. B.Richard

3. D.He doesn't wear pants

4. A.True

5. D.Mexican food

6. C.Carrie

7. A.True

8. D.Ukulele

9. C.Feathers

10. A.Cat

11. C.Blue

12. D.Pink

13. A.True

14. C.38

15. A.True

16. C.November 1st

17. B.B

18. C.November 12th

19. A.True

20. D.Rabbit

21. C.6

22. D.All of the above

23. A.True

24. B.Sausage

25. A.True

DID YOU KNOW?

➤ The character Richard Watterson was originally written as a dog.

➤ Darwin is also based on Ben Bocquelet's long-time friend Paul.

➤ The three sets of doors at the entrance of Gumball's school represent the colors of Anais, Gumball, and Darwin: pink, blue, and orange.

CHAPTER 6

SEE YOU LATER

LET'S QUIZZ!

1. In "The Man," Richard is shown to be able to play the guitar.

    A. True

    B. False

2. He can speak ____ fluently as revealed in "The Remote."

    A. France

    B. Chinese

    C. Spanish

    D. Japanese

3. Penny is in the school's cheer leading team.

    A. True

    B. False

4. How old is Penny?

    A. 12

    B. 14

    C. 16

    D. 18

5. Who is Penny's father?

    A. Andy

    B. Arthur

    C. Thor

    D. Patrick

6. Who is Penny's mother?

    A. Judith

    B. Anna

    C. Annie

    D. Katy

7. Who is Penny's younger sister?

    A. Peni

    B. Polly

    C. Poy

    D. Punny

8. What is Penny's pet name?

    A. Mr. Cindy

    B. Mr. Candy

    C. Mr. Cuddles

    D. Mr. Chanmy

9. What color is Penny's pet?

    A. Black

    B. Brown

    C. Blue

    D. Yellow

10. How many eyes does Penny's pet have?

    A. 2

    B. 4

    C. 6

    D. 8

11. What color is Mr. Cuddles's eyes?

 A. Blue

 B. Brown

 C. Black

 D. Red

12. Mr. Cuddles is a tarantula.

 A. True

 B. False

13. How old is Carrie Krueger?

 A. 123

 B. 324

 C. 327

 D. 400

14. What is Carrie Krueger's species?

 A. Cat

 B. Ghost

 C. Fish

 D. Horse

15. Penny is very nice and friendly.

   A. True

   B. False

16. Who is the person that Carrie is dating?

   A. David

   B. Gumball

   C. Darwin

   D. No one

17. How old is Tobias Wilson?

   A. 10

   B. 12

   C. 14

   D. 16

18. What is Tobias Wilson's species?

   A. Rainbow lad

   B. Cloudy lad

   C. Rainy lad

   D. Windy lad

19. Penny is also very sensitive, as she can be easily hurt.

   A. True

   B. False

20. Who is Tobias's mother?

   A. Annie

   B. Jackie

   C. Anna

   D. Stella

21. Who is Tobias's father?

   A. Daniel

   B. Louis

   C. Harry

   D. Harold

22. Carrie was dating Azrael for one to _____

   A. two decades

   B. three decades

   C. four decades

   D. five decades

23. Penny is the only member of her family to have broken out of her shell.

    A. True

    B. False

24. What is Carrie's gender?

    A. Male

    B. Female

25. Carrie can't hold and manipulate physical objects with her hands.

    A. True

    B. False

CHAPTER 6

SEE YOU LATER

ANSWERS ARE COMING!!

1. A.True

2. C.Spanish

3. A.True

4. A.12

5. D.Patrick

6. A.Judith

7. B.Polly

8. C.Mr. Cuddles

9. A.Black

10. C.6

11. D.Red

12. A.True

13. C.327

14. B.Ghost

15. A.True

16. C.Darwin

17. B.12

18. A.Rainbow lad

19. A.True

20. B.Jackie

21. D.Harold

22. A.two decades

23. A.True

24. B.Female

25. B.False

DID YOU KNOW?

- Carrie the Ghost is in 3-D if you put on 3-D glasses.
- Gumball, Darwin, and Anais are the only child characters to be voiced by actual kids.
- In the show, it is revealed that the last name of Carrie is Kruger which makes her name a "Double Homage" to two Horror characters. Her First Name to Stephen King's character "Carrie" and her Last Name to "Nightmare on Elm Street" character Freddie Kruger.

Made in the USA
Columbia, SC
16 May 2023

16759788R00036